VESTIGES

Poems by

Bill F. Ndi

Langaa Research & Publishing CIG
Mankon, Bamenda

Publisher:
Langaa RPCIG
Langaa Research & Publishing Common Initiative Group
P.O. Box 902 Mankon
Bamenda
North West Region
Cameroon
Langaagrp@gmail.com
www.langaa-rpcig.net

Distributed in and outside N. America by African Books Collective
orders@africanbookscollective.com
www.africanbookcollective.com

ISBN: 9956-728-64-0

DISCLAIMER
All views expressed in this publication are those of the author and do
not necessarily reflect the views of Langaa RPCIG.

Author's Note

This Collection is what it is; a skeleton. Bring on the flesh.

Bill F. Ndi

To my beloved fun loving brother Sammy Sunny Ndi who departed to rest in the Lord on January 24th, 2013.

Table of Contents

Our Rooftop Catacombs... 1

Big World, Small Talk... 2

Disposition/This Position! 2

Pens I've Held.. 5

Death's Fame... 5

Age.. 6

Dictatorship.. 6

My Finding...7

In the deeps... 8

What Use? 9

Pilgrims' Evergreen... 10

At table.. 11

This Burning Desire.. 13

Waiting for a Call... 14

Crazy Carpet... 14

The Whiskers... 15

Flirt in Flight..16

The Wings... 16

Wholly Whole... 17

Pin in Their heart.. 17

Downsizing... 18

Roonians' Home.. 19

My Shirt.. 19

In a Trap? 20

I Am Proud... 21

Gusty Winds.. 23

Draught...24

My Fantasy...25

Sun Rays... 25

The Bang.. 26
Falstaff Bastille Souvenir.......................... 27
Commitment : Tender's Key....................... 27
Cleansing Droplets................................... 28
Migrants.. 28
Heart.. 29
Po Eh Tree.. 30
Spelling Victory...................................... 31
Scarecrow.. 32
Nimbus, My Cry...................................... 32
From Inside-out...................................... 33
Hanging Tulip... 34
A Find? 35
Thirst Quenching.................................... 36
Dear Mourner.. 37
Little Imp.. 38
Clan of Skunks....................................... 39
Those Dreams.. 40
The Weapons... 41
Auto-Critique (Then and Now).................. 41
Their Pen... 42
The Throes.. 43
Loving Mums... 44
Notes to Keep Afloat.............................. 48
A Train Ride From Paris X Nanterre........... 49
Digger Digger... 49
Their Gift to Us...................................... 50
Old Boys' Story....................................... 51
Agony Free Freedom............................... 52
Daddy Sixty... 53
That's Him... 53
Lives in My Head.................................... 54

The Jewel.. 55
Bitter Pill.. 55
As the World Goes Round.. 56
My Here and There.. 57
Stirrer... 58
Farewell.. 59
Farewell II... 60
Farewell III.. 61
Farewell IV.. 62
Farewell V... 63
Farewell VI.. 64
Farewell VII... 65
Farewell VIII.. 66
Marshals in the Marshes... 67
May Tree... 68
Class of 84.. 69
A Hopeful's Day.. 70
Spare Me... 71
Portuguese Lobster.. 72
Won't Sink in Sync... 72
With the Sails Set.. 73
Where the Ravens Gloat.. 74
Brides of Gold.. 76
This Dark World…! 77
P5 & 8.. 78

Our Rooftop Catacombs

01/02-07/10

Where I sit to give flesh to dry bones in poetry,
I give all hand to come stand on Mahogany
Then feast their eyes on my ailing father's mansion
'Tis such none can rescue with any injection.
This ailment upheld by sloths feeding fat on dates,
Busy at work against the hopes we have on our slate:
To retell our sleeping mount Fako of his birth
To dig out all that which this calabash holds, death.
He is all the dregs in to sprout shoots of misery
With lengthy motions in hope to sit in history
And not in the memory our people have of him
As one who wrecks their hopes and makes power his
                                 whim
To which as censors poets refuse to beat their brow
Yet, those of the herded scribes would go for the here
                             and now
And cast our monster in a mould of abiliment
In a rampage as they do crave part in government
Not one by the people but one on them imposed
To leave father's house with skeletal overdose
And a king and his, mentally and morally
With our people and their kin in ruin haplessly;
Such flag bearers flag up the need for the big tree
From which to see our abode blooms with leafless trees.

Big World, Small Talk

From work, I go home.
From work, I walk home.
Home I go to walk
To rest from small talk.
Small talk their big world
Would with make big words.

07 Feb. 2010

Disposition/This Position!

Keep your money
Keep your trophies
Keep your glories
See me happy
And let my life
Without a strife,
Without wings I'd
Fly sky high! You'd
Ask what on earth
Saddens you; dearth
Of my sadness
Leaves you a mess
Sends you raging
With you screaming
Your madness for
The listed four:
Money, trophies,
Sadness, glories,
Your soul's desire
Birthing quagmire.

You my foes know
I know your woes:
This greed you breed
Won't let you breathe.
Wanting my life?
Your goal in life!
A step so bold
To steal the gold
Nature's given;
You need taken
Away from me
To make of me
Wan and wretched
Yet, styled wicked
In which world dons
Glow without fun.
In their bastions?
Generations
Left to themselves,
Help fill the shelves;

Those of misery
Wiping memory
Off the pages.
Human pages
Burnt to ashes
For being witches.
Hunting this witch
We'll make a stitch
With a penned verse
That will reverse
This diffused brain

That's put more strain
On our beauty
And we're not free
Till happiness
Knocks your madness.
Won't you accept
Such an excerpt
To put an end
To your mad trend?

11 Feb. 2010

Pens I've Held

Some pens I held did not disappoint me
And some let me sting; I stung like a bee.
Yet, the sweetness that of them came made sense
To those who sweetness desire and sentence
To a life of pain, those who with us toyed
And on our life's paths their armies deployed.
To these foes? A life of making money!
For us? It's been a life to make honey!
What in mind they have is not sanity
Pushing them to slaughter for safety
So they say, or our lives won't be safe
Just to make away with what's in our safe
Fronting peaceful pens with their warring guns
Yet, these pens will live to pen many puns.

10 Feb 2010

Death's Fame

Knowing all your fame over our life is fake
Why should I, death, wear a wrinkle for your sake?
Before J. D. said you shall die, you had died
A fact known to all you'd really like to hide
For a fame that's all lame and everyone knows;
Stunted with no one at all to say it grows.
Maybe for the coward still squirming thoughtlessly,
In whose little minds you farm fear ceaselessly.

Age

Till I rest, I shall not fold into two.
Many a weak spirits you've reduced too.
Turning their sweet dreams about life all stale
With signs leaving none blind to their tall tale
Of the rugged sea in which they have swum
With some rougher; yet, that won't mine benumb
Being a well designed story with rebounds
Won't it, drag yours for sure, straight to the grounds?

10 Feb. 2010

Dictatorship

A bunch of babbling jargon speaking lunatics
Penury dictates what some call charismatic
When they talk. In tongues they say they talk as if toes
Others use to talk. They point Friends' silence as woes.
Yet, popular dictum paints silence as golden
While for them babbling in tongues is ultra modern;
Such demagogues would blend and spice their sweet
                                                                promises
That give a lustre to their grip on the masses
Seeing in them such articulateness unheard
Of by any of the cows that flock in such herd
Grazing under the falling goad of the head man
For grace to avoid his ire against their demand
For what from birth is a birth right none should reject
Or, as those behind goat head do their own neglect.

17 Feb. 2010

My Finding

Once was I told: Happiness
Had enemies. Bitterness
I found an arch enemy
Killing and without mercy
This gloss of all souls alive.
Why with this rake wreck your life?
Bury bitterness and grow
Happiness and you will glow
In the darkness bitterness
Projects to slay happiness!

18/02/2010

In the deeps

It was my favourite transport system.
I didn't know it was a home.
And I sought after that!
And found it filled with just those
For a mental home good!
Ask me not where?
Ask me not which deeps?
It was in Paris!
I won't say in the metro!
You don't know
What this is? I'll say,
In England we call it "tube"
Subvert it not for a cube!
Else you'll be used in a soup
To savour the tongues that taste French
Tasty mustard from Burgundy.

Desolate eyes on lifeless faces plugged
At one another peering as if drugged
To plug life off the others; tube ride on
And as peering or piercing does plod on
Down the deep entrails of the bleak subway
Such is life there and that's the only way!
Was once told to pack bag and baggage
Which was a fancy to calm a pen in rage
Such rage the pen needs for its thoughts so deep
And back in the deeps there's no way he'd sleep.

What Use?

By my grave the cow grazes!
In life I didn't need praises
Some would want to sing for me
As I've kissed death than freely
They would have when I was strong
With every move they saw wrong
Why stir the air they did chill?
Why worry? Leave it up hill!
For down the grave one needs calm
And praises won't be the balm.

Pilgrims' Evergreen

On a grim land these grim pilgrims grin
At their dreamland coloured evergreen
The painter's brush had left them to hope
In that land, their tears will never rope
Down their cheeks as has been forced to flood
And drown all hopeful whose stolen nod
Beamed with all but grin at promises
Schemes soon extinct in the premises
In which unclad shamans display might
And reign sitting on the pilgrims' plight:
Grim or green. What matters is these *lords'*
Disdain leaving the world short of words
But not those to point out the foibles
In which lords bathe at dinner table
For their belly's first, for the rest? Bones!
To show around and just fleshless bones!

At table

Father cut a piece of cheese and all sniffed it
Knowing not where to put those noses that sniffed it
It was evidence he is bloating fart on milk
That crafts his body smooth, soft and shiny like silk.

Before then, the cake all hungrily hoped appeared,
He pushed down into his belly with no crumbs spared
For the tiny lads whose dreams were to pick them up
And fertilize their slim skinny hopes to grow up

Around which table the cult expects them to crawl
For such within are sights that kiss bliss and enthrall
Leaving this jerk a smirk of a sneak from a brothel;
So, quest not which for none would be the one to tell.

He's espoused a hussy with whom he feeds all thin
And leaves just no flesh to their barebones but the skin
Whose lofty images colour screens and hound favour
That project so much holdup in their endeavour

For they are panhandling lepers with nothing more
Not even blood in their veins that would bless the gore
To appease the ghouls of his brothel; no! Palace
Queen bringing all abjection! And to him solace....

Long shall they at this table dine shielded by vice
Knowing not they, not the people, will pay the price
For forfeiture lousily indulged in, in life
Letting the demon himself take them for a drive.

They enjoy maiming the world with total misery
Which when asked to redress, they view as foolery
And would requesters their lives surrender to them
For not all must be those to sit and steer the helm.

Sleazy helm claimants need not; but a better stead
Which must be sought after without receiving death
That's the lot today and come shall come that day
When the tides will turn and all shall receive their pay.

And in their graves frost bites they'll receive and not rice
On which alive they fed fat ignoring our cries
Of the pangs hunger dealing blows to our stomachs
While theirs and their queens' needed not an almanac.

This Burning Desire

What I won't do!
That she won't do!
In this plane I want;
No, my heart pants
'n would I gave a pass
To a bony lass
With just one eye!
Blink? How could I?
I have Motrin
Sentient K trine
Who has just Bill
Think what they will!
I will not pretend.
K trine, I contend:
"K trine is all!"
Makes my man tall
And in this craft
For her I'm aft
With my drumming heart
Drumming a music
A music that speaks
Peak love to my heart.

Waiting for a Call

Travelling through Charles De Gaulle
I stood sweating for this call
Whence my eyes caught travelers
Who were on the spot dreamers
For an escapade they'd fly
While with the means they'll comply
Never. Such dregs none drinks
For 'twixt dregs and drunks no links
Link them for there is a blind
Leaving one class in a bind
One in which in pain they pine
While on the spot their travails shine
And glisten with rays finely tuned;
With past, present and future pruned!

Crazy Carpet

07/03/2010

Sure ! Happily all slept on that grass mattress !
Yes, all did! Yet, did trade it all blind for stress
On this hanging floor with its mad plastic rug
For which before, all were all high as on drug
Trading their buttresses for this better life
Tapping honey by stinging bees in their hive!
Quiet hive like honey bee sting devoid of pain?
That in that cart brought man to hunt hope for gain
And to drag all down downhill this muddy slope;
Now in the valley all only strive to cope!

14

The Whiskers

07/03/2010

Growing up seeing
Scarred faces taking
Kids to graves, rang no bell
Of our homestead oil well,
Her mine fields being scars
Here on earth not Mars
Like whiskers standing
Straight and unbending

Dug up for her dust
All driven by lust;
If hell wishes, greed
That leaves mauls that bleed
Broken virgin empty.
Scoring mark? Hefty!
If not bleed of mud
Like this unblessed mud
Some hand some to drink
We revert with ink

Flirt in Flight

07/03/2010

Sand storm in their desert
This man and this woman
About to give each a pass
With only a glance
Leave the fruit on trees hanging
In case of crash
Will they lovers
End up in heaven?
Or bitter enemies
Still good friends
For not consuming
Such lusty love looks
In pretty little minds buried?

The Wings

07/03/2010

Flapping those broken wings
Faster than would go flying
Sings for some wisdom song
Birds glide and sing no wrong
Making landing goal whole
Short cut? Cut short no soul
Birds their pace keep from prey;
Huntsmen to snatch birds' pray!

Wholly Whole

07-14/03/2010

Two sides to every story.
Silence completes no story.
When you take freedom
Prick not at random.
Flowery silence drums
These big conundrums.

The wind with all might
Has come for a fight
No one is told why
And with eyes we buy
Hers and with silence
Hold it evidence….

Pin in Their heart

07/03/2010

Mass grave skeletons
In cupboards weigh tons
And rattle songs unsung
To drum their ears with wrong
Big fat snitch serves as key
To pull green hands a quay
Whereon the jag digs mass graves
For a world both new and brave.

Downsizing

08/03/2010

We too shrink everyday.
The world does.
So does World Company.

We are boxed faraway
Just like dross
That no eye wants to see.

Even furthermost on the fringes
Of their shrunken world without bridges
To that abysm which drinks us up

In which our thinned bones would not fill up;
Not with us by the zillion infinities
On which scene alight crack heads' infirmities.

Roonians' Home

11/03/2010

Sweaty drips perfume her subways
And dog pooh litter her pathways
Such C. T. Roonians call home
And would trade that home for Rome
Neither home nor Rome baits this heart.
In either, pierced by a dart
From the heartless slaughtering freedom
In abattoirs built on huge slums.

My Shirt

11/03/2010

My crystal white shirt I don't want stained
Begs deterrence from the police
With Sparkles that rain negation;
Shirts need be soiled to gain protection.
Law and order means crime first
Laden coffins put to rest
With accusation coming
In droves and their blames falling?

In a Trap?

11/03/2010

Hate told big fat lies I fell in a trap
And though on the face I've received a slap
I know full well Peace will light up the way
And a smile shall bloom at the dawn of May
So shall Peace and Love embrace happiness
Grinding policing into nothingness
One must keep watering this flowery garden
In whose dust man's does return to Eden!
Stop man not! Man or hate! That will all fail
As for real, LOVE shall distance fairytale!

I Am Proud

Death you make me proud!
And stack me a crowd!
With your bees to sting,
With your snakes biting,
Where gloating vultures,
Beacon dream matures
For thirsty leeches
With lengthy speeches
To convince sucking
As good as docking
A ship a strange port
Being the best of sport.

Death, must I wear pride,
My gown like a bride's
Snow pure with whiteness
You don't want to witness
Goaded it's my dream
Drowning me down stream
With you oblivious
But flagging devious
Incisors to blight
Innocence at night
Whence you shall fall short
And shall face the odd?

Why should I be pricked?
I know yours all bleak!
I wake up bemused.
Your dreams are reduced
Tatters to ribbon
Bits tickling gibbons
Screaming off their lungs
Chanting happy songs
Lulling baby me
With no busy bee
To steal or kill my
Calm near where you lie.

Lie. Yes! Death you lie!
Life shall live not die!
Returns I've witnessed
Table you slyness
Slicing in halves grains
Men sow for great gains
With thoughts such a fall
Shall make you stand tall
The height above you
I see soaring too
Lifting up my heart
As you fall apart.

Gusty Winds

The wind rushed to us
Bringing along frost
Not our longing
Nor our yearning;
Falling down trees
Downing houses
And stilling lives
Cut from the hives
Blown by this gust
Scattering the crust
From stinking cheese
By jagged sleeves
Sending out jitters
With hopes they slither
We sent back with frown
Seeing the shark crowned
Teeth with their laugh
As they won't starve
As we won't eye
But slap them bye!

Draught

16/03/2010

Draught from that tap
Beacons rag-tag
For this draught flows
On raining blows
Chiseling so hard
One must be mad
To drink such draught
And make no draft
To crack open
Dungeons for men
To breathe fresh air
Stroking their hair
Pumping their lungs
To singing songs.

My Fantasy

28/03/2010

I have been fantasizing
About cigarette smoking
No about cigars and hemp
Seeing myself kissing them
Yet, they'd wait till my clock strike

Ninety! Then I'd start a strike
When death and dying mean nothing
Smoking hell out of smoking
With cigarettes, cigars and hemp
That'll the long sleeves of life hem.

Sun Rays

28/03/2010

Big bright Sun, cold or hot
I'm butter in a pot
And would melt under heat
With no drop staining sheets
Of this love that's so pure.
To forgive? A real cure!

The Bang

28/03/2010

The doors have just shot
And I feel I'm caught
When for real, I'd been blind
To think that love, a find.

In cage, freedom void
With the spy police deployed
To butcher everything
Trust did in confiding

Blindly faithfully too
When to tango takes two
With both in love and blind
That won't each other grind.

Falstaff Bastille Souvenir

27/03/2010

Paris night life stretched a hand
Which to grab, made me in Falstaff land!
Tired of drinking
A bang on the table
Shouted: "you must
Sit up and play the game!"
That of capital
Reproduction; consume!
More drinks till you drop
And drop they won't let one drop!
For if these leaves leave trees
Falling off host branches
They'd bury capital under
Not with a strike of thunder.

Commitment : Tender's Key

Round the globe I trotted for five years.
Came back. Same old tender told me yes!
With this key he unlocked one true sense.
One conjugated not in past tense
But past, present and future tenses
For which to see, none needed lenses.
His position was, is and will be
Sweet and even sweeter than honey!

Cleansing Droplets

02/04/2010

Mustering their force and marching down stream
Cleansing water droplets knead a dream
Sweeping away debris they have piled
Which all, after yearning, reviled.

With sparkles clean now, all these kin
Fattened with manure won't be thin
And would bloom and blossom like spring
Without need to be of the ring.

Migrants

Tree leaves blown here and there
Leave the trees there not here.
The roots such leaves should feed;
Wounded trees left to bleed!
The station unchanged, cloak
Those trees with a new coat
Wanderers wear to sing big
With words that neither dig
Nor bury big fat lies
In this world needing ties
Words won't dig to bury
My grating live story.

Heart

This thumping heart,
The feet of air
Moves and sets
In motions
Some heartbeats'
Swords after
Hearts;
To stop them.

In rage they drive
In without care
Thumping heart
Flower rose
The right dose
Unwelcomed
By green eyed
Big Ogre.

Po Eh Tree

I am not a protestant
I am not a protester
I am protest itself born
Who'd stand up for his kin wrung!

Po eh tree won't be coaxed
Knowing you have hoaxed
And spited the kind, fools
And trampled upon rules,

Picked up roses in hate,
Using roses as bait!
To prick with pin sharp thorns
Not the promise of corns.

Spelling Victory

Flowing   from   those   taps   by   the   Mungo
Framed *circuits*, tracks on which slowly grow
Fossilizing dead brains renowned drunk
And stuck with stinking fart from skunks
Skunks use to mark their territory
Staggering with feverish victory
Sending the stench of dead rat
Hitting   hard all little brat
Taking pride in night flight
Apprehensive   of   trite
Choir masters intone
With hammers on stone
Racking brains
Pouring rains
From eyes
On   ice
G r i p
Drip
I
I
I
!
!
Want to see liquid
Or you should just quit

So none would see *mimbo* in a cup
That has been giving us the hiccup.

Scarecrow

In tatters, such scarecrow scares
And grips poets' pens in nightmares
Not the poet taking head on
Medusa and riding on
Skeletally spiked pavement
Spiting anything payment
'Cos in poets' hand all pens right
The wrongs about which they write!

Nimbus, My Cry

My dark cries the like of nimbus bring rain
If dickhead hears not all my cries the rain
Will hit him hard as hail and he will feel
These long years he has spooled mine on a reel
With jollity and merry-going-round
To bury facts for the grave all are bound
As my pens weep not only for his plight
But laugh at caitiffs putting up big fights
For the glorification of such goats
Who with their kind on rough sea rock the boats
Then jump up and down with flags of success
With all else going adrift in recess.

From Inside-out

27/04/2010

My love slaps the face stark naked!
Isn't she beauty dressed naked?
Only uncouth eyes would away
Shy from such a spell whose sway
Makes shrubs grow baobab branches;
Big love size winters won't freeze.

Hanging Tulip

'Twixt the arches
Perch tulip leaves
Mouth wide open
This hot oven
Soothing a loaf
Bait to a dove
Flying away
To keep at bay
Trouble waters
Tulip slayers
To stir give vent
Without talent
Devoid of sparks
From singing larks
Letting blizzards
Beating lizards
To drum praises
As time races
Towards dry bones
That would spite scones!

23/04/2010

A Find?

When I found a carcass
My eyes went after the essence
Which this living carcass
Did pride take in intelligence

Ousting the light that would shine
Above the monstrous black city sky
Scuttling across the grapevine
This sour truth to which men must comply;

Part! Should men plod away
Leaving behind flesh and bone for worms
To feed on anyway
Without ever nursing thoughts of drums?

Thirst Quenching

To warrant all have their rights
After war faring with guns
Pens anger grips together crumbs
And sends home to rest from fights

Pens do bleed bitterness sweet
The likes of palm tree syrup sweet
Bled from the wounds of a cut
With a smooth sail down the gut.

With a smirk all will be fine
In the evening all will dine
And have sips of this syrup
After which they'll sit up.

Dear Mourner

Please! Shed no tears
I had no fears
This long legged day
Would sojourn this way
And bring peace to a soul
All along restless whole
In rave brave and grave
Smiling villain's knave
And spiting long life
Diehards who clench to life
And letting nothing
Go! Power? Their thing?
With guns to spark fears?
My pen does wipe tears
Tears none need to shed
Where Sophia is bred
Her insight well groomed
I'd be boxed and roomed
Where I'd be landlord
With no mourning word
From my lonely love
For whom flies my dove.

Little Imp

12.4.10-03.5.10 & 12.6.10

You rose like the Sun
Of whom we thought well
Knowing you a son
Of the soil whose bell
Sound would the mountain
Bring down to the plain
To an abode make
For national cake
Watering appetite
Growing not our plight
Dressing roads with rocks
Creating stumbling blocks
For all aspirants
Far from resilient
Wanting your sunset
Blowing a trumpet
To send you back home!
Deserve you a home?
Hell, you fashioned ours
In matter of hours!
And out here we stray
While at home you prey
To glaze your wrinkle
Leaving no sprinkle
To the thirsty bloke
Asking not for coke
But understanding
From one whose standing
Replicates sun's rays

And not your mad plays
That end up killing
The kind and willing.
Little imp goodbye!
We all know you'll die!

Clan of Skunks

18/03/2010

On the roof tops they sit
And the houses smell shit
And with pride they slay time
With all left without dime
Till lightening grabs his sword
To pronounce the last word
With new lungs breathing fresh
Mint, smoothening sloppy flesh
Skunks would love to nibble
Same as they would dwindle
State coffers, lifting debt
Before lying in bed
With our bones on the streets
Eager to trick skunks treats.

Those Dreams

13th May 10

We had dreams;
Then we were young.
Drank from streams
Were told we're wrong.
Yet, steam, our dream
Gave life this beam
We've thus followed
In this boat rowed
With great efforts
Needing no forts
For protection
Nor solution
But dreams
Upstream.

The Weapons

14/05/10

Poets have just words
To bury swords
Twisted 'n forged with lies
Founding human cries.

Auto-Critique (Then and Now)

12/05/2010

Our childhood, was it in opulence
Brought or brought to strive at excellence?
Dream most of us did and do espouse
Amidst many a blood sucking louse
Sucking from inside-out every drop!
Won't we now quest why all won't say stop
To all these leeches in opulence
Swimming and rummaging excellence?
Even as their strength from outside comes
With their virtue of vice breeding harms
Yet, we have the last word and must air
To embrace such weather that's all fair.

Their Pen

They have just one pen
Who points to a den
With hungry lions infested
Dreaming he'd be ingested.
Yet, the pen stands its ground
With his ink, have lions drowned
In a sea of steel strong words
Throwing lions overboard
And with his nip like a spear
Does prick bringers of despair
And turns its back from power
Cherished by misery grower
Which does himself see a goad
Thoughtless to all he's a load
They know not what to do with;
Was he thus groomed in the heath?
Does poets' pen not tell us this?
"By the den, there is no bliss."

The Throes

23/05/10

The old lady acquiesced! Nodded! Then a smile!
In the metro, this couple blew their kiss a mile
And cracked open buds of roses with a bolt! Told?
Yes, not everywhere! But in Paris, 'tis retold!
A sight to prod one to see this city and die!
Here, I see love and laugh as love does the most cry
To paint the clowns' smiling face with inks of sadness.
From within? Gloom! From without? Posted happiness!
This broadens kids' smile with this lady's in the metro
With delights to see arrows fly out from a bow.

Loving Mums

Paris, May 2010 Mothers Day

When I would I came to this world,
Who was there to take me in?
That was mum!

When my foetus would it were incubated,
Who stood the heat for nine long months?
You bet, that was mum!

When I kicked in changes in hormones,
Who could for months stand this?
With patience, full of hopes, mum did!

When I fought my way into this weird world and caused
                                              pain,
Who cried and cried out for joy and ignored the pain?
Without any question, my mum!

When I cried at birth,
Who stood there and sang for me?
That was mum!

When hunger had its grip on me,
Who fed me?
I say my mum!

When I tried to take my first steps,
Who held my hands so I didn't fall?
Certainly my mum did!

When I was growing up and got hurt,
Was there any to look after me?
Yes! For sure, mum was there!

When I needed fees,
Who did I see for these?
That was mum!

So, when stubbornness raged in,
Who whipped up discipline?
A gain my mum!

When bad boys company I kept,
Who my attention drew?
Just my mum!

When penury came with notes of exploitation,
Who refused to play drums for this stranger?
Indeed my mum did!

When we craved a special dish,
Who made us feast?
Who else but sweet mum?

When at nights mares came in,
Who else could hunt down our fears?
It was none but mum!

Mum here, mum there
Ubiquitous mum!
Rechristened Mami Rubber!

In Africa, in America.
With her rubber she kept the line straight
For sure, across the world

When I queried what penury said,
What did mum have to say?
She would at midnight rooftops fly!

When I questioned why?
Her chords greeted my ears with,
"The unseen. Mums wield power!"

When I slew time,
Who told me about a stitch in time?
That was mum!

When I thought I should laze around,
Who laid the foundation of hard work?
Query not this. It was my mum!

When in sick bed and doctors thought me dead,
Who prayed and said they were wrong?
My mum did and she was right!

When I shouldered leeches home,
Who sucked them out of me?
If not my mum, then I am wrong!

When the world weighed me down,
Who lifted up my soul with songs of praise?
I will still tell you, that was mum!

When dads flopped in their roles,
Who wore the crowns of thorns?
Sure not dads but mums!

Were mum alive and I died,
Who would mourn the most?
Nobody but mum who's always been there!

Even when I wounded myself and bled
You won't believe who sobbed!
Both my mum and my step mum!

When I quested where they their bitterness kept,
None would guess what I was told,
I was their child and must stay out of their fight!

So, as I plodded West, questions on me hailed!
They inquired about my mum
And cheerfully, I talked of my mums!

Curious listeners laughed out their lungs
And would hang me with one last question! Mums?
Yes! Every Woman in my home is a mother

Notes to Keep Afloat

This soul came from far away
With Spring giving Summer way
And at Montparnasse, the Paris subway
With nothing but his saxophone to play

He blasted his best shots!
They did well! Stroke the chords.
First, having all heads in the train nod
With this strike on the keys to have blood

Flow, flowing gently down the deep
Then sending their little hands deep
Into their pockets wherein heaps
Of raw change laze like elves asleep

Those without which happily some will deal
Only glad to hear such call for a meal
With: he just called to say, he loves…! To steal
All attention in caves with a skill

Which back home he pined and pined with in vain
And dreamt and dreamt Paris that mountain train
In which these notes he would strike to kill pain
Taking him places, the like of this train…

A Train Ride From Paris X Nanterre

The train stopped on the platform.
We hurried in, top in form!
A can cracked and woke me up!
And my head I lifted up;
All I saw was a young man
Over whom drink had command.
He drank and drank life away
And kept my mouth wide open!
I looked at my watch? Seven!
And his liquid slime breakfast
Thus comes first leaving him last
Not close to his least worries
About us cooking stories.

Digger Digger

Peak axes prick the soil
To feed her with some spoils
Which colour homeland red
And sticks out without dread;
Blossoms of polished crime,
A rhyme with homeland clime
Where from these sighs we heave
Wherein we're left to grieve.

Their Gift to Us

With our hands tied, they spoon feed us pain.
We bathe in pain and they reap their gain.
Yet, the cry we cry shall their songs be
That'll sing in their ears tinnitus bee.

To free the free bird in us fee free
To fly sky high and perch on a tree
In their world they call free; free to trade
As in the years of yore they did trade

My kind of yore their merchandise was
Their unkind heart beat and did far worse
Till machines gain pricked them at conscience
To show humaneness as a new science

And whitewash the blood stain of their deed
A deed that's all been guided by greed
And today accounts for us tied up
And beaten as we boycott their shop

Old Boys' Story

Seventy years ago, that was then
They felt free far from fried chicken
And what's the story seventy years after?
While window shopping they crouched to the counter!

A weird thing! Were all these years spent on the spot
The hands of life would have made such a big shot
Cherished and pampered, coveted and cuddled
Being the living and walking book not muddled.

Herewith seventy years gone straight near a bin
Oblivious all else would be swept by the wind
With seventy years of sunset blown away
Like dust in a tornado rushed faraway

Far, far away from home where these grains of dust
Dance round and round in search of a handsome crust
On which to sit their bump and contemplate life
That in this whirlwind has seen turbulence rife.

Here we flame and burn in the Diaspora,
Such dreams in many a sound sleep flower
To birth fate against which we'd turn our backs
To fly sky high and cruise on the right tracks

Agony Free Freedom

29/06/2010

You see? The worst still to come!
I'd rather covet the calm
Of today than agonise
And kill a day blessed so nice!

How would fear and worry change
Such cast moulded to be strange
If one stood or ran away
From blood bath rife either way?

Here or across those bridges
You'd come by such stooges;
They'd surround you either way
With readiness to betray

The calm you would came with joy
Sleeps not with their thoughtless ploy
To see you frantic and mad
About them pricking you sad

With slogans the worst is still
To pop up and from you still
The agony free freedom
Promised as a New Kingdom.

Daddy Sixty

01/07/2010

Too late
To hate
With drooped open mouth just watch oldies
Here at Chatelet-les-Halles; they simulate
Youths every here and there in baggies
Would that reduced their age! Too late!
Again,
A gain?

Too late
To state
They have come short of the glory of age
As they strive to put our youths off their stage
With no thoughts in ours we fought to be free
From robes of constraints worn on liberty,
The grain
We gain!

That's Him

You'd go round the whole world
One you'd find summed in a word.
He means the whole world and Fonya
His name! For the meaning? Go to Africa!

Lives in My Head

No doubt!
I know!
All know
And proud
That great lives bustle in my head
Which to see one needs a head
And two eyes to read
These lines from a reed
Dropped to jot a point
That miseries anoint
And grace the thin skin of earth
Whose plight is blessed without mirth
In my head, in my world one dream
Shall come and shall flow like a stream
Bathe the banks clean from mud
Ready the ground for buds;
Flower buds that'll tell stories
Ours will be with no worries
Just no worries from gangsters
Who deprive us of lobsters,
Delicacies for those mouths
Who entwine lies so uncouth
And make Paris the jewel
In whom all would fare just well.

19/07/10

The Jewel

Paris, the jewel and pride of modernity
This same Paris is the cradle of liberty;
Such dream had by many a million
To see her and die without mention
Yet, she leaves mankind with much to desire
With everything humaneness down in the mire
For the West, primitiveness at work
Tells the story why one would mock
This jewel of the western mind
At display of all that's unkind.

22/07/10

Bitter Pill

The subway swarmed with the world,
Her eyes the red of her pants
Streaming tears and helpless
By they who cared less,
In which blues she saw red
While all whisked by her and sped
I stopped to give a hug
In hope I chased her pain away
And heard her say,
"My brother lay dying!"
A wave through me echoing,
"You'll be all right!"
Then I wiped her tears.
They ran a chill,

Such chill down my poor spine
With which I plodded away
Weighted down by deep pain
With just one wish
I would I could
Whisk it off
Never to see
Eyes so teary.

Paris, Chatelet, 22/07/10

As the World Goes Round

2/08/2010

Places, things and people
Never seen
Never ceased to be
Thanks to ignorance;
They're there or here.
The world goes round.
The Sun slaves everyday
From East to West
After that old tradition: Wisdom
Not the priorities of their kingdom!

My Here and There

11/08/10

When I left home, I headed for somewhere
I would it was home when I got there.
There I am neither there nor here;
My idyll's far from here and there.

My essence drove into a brain
And brought with it hopes in its train
And did aim to peak the mountain
Whereon resides no ache and pain.

At the end of the day here lie
The remnants of he who did vie
And sounded own trumpet to fly
Away with no wings but my pie.

With my pie away, should I chase
Its shadow to such a strange place
Where my eyes burst at a weird face
For which they did not themselves brace?

Stirrer

12/09/10

I rode from Fumban
Towards Bangolan
With splendid nature
My eyes do treasure
Tainted by gendarmes
Who stretch their long arms
To which I'd not stoop
But jump all their hoops
Put along the course
To muzzle the cause
I pray all took home
And of it make chrome
Not the Blood red thirst
For which they are first!

Farewell

12/09/10

It was April, I last saw daddy!
Dad was about to leave his body
In hospital bed! He took my hand
Which he squeezed and squeezed hard with his hand
And mused we'd scream out loud in August!
I dreamt we'd with joy do come August!
Then he entered me as I was blank
Knowing not come August he'd be plank
And have our tears wash the stele
He'd have us erect with none to feel
That August of my nativity
Be August of his mortality.
Yet, both death and birth come August
I thus embrace the two as life's trust!

Farewell II

19/09/10

My hand? Dad gripped hard never to let go!
And when I left he knew he had to go!
And left words behind for a wanderer
Who'd so become come early September
When a new ridge would grace with awe the piece
Given him to administer in Peace
And call all heads to drop as they pass by
In this journey for which they would not vie
Now I know the ultimate end of time
So close that one never gets to its prime
By our own measure by which we assume
In plenty we have nothing to consume
The infiniteness of it though finite
With more than half spent with our tears glossed plight.

Farewell III

10/04/10

Down there, daddy is strong and carries
All by himself, an obelisk that's his
And tells his story as a soldier
Who fought a fight, though not a ranger,
With his wisdom to kids to challenge
Their anger with calm void of revenge
And such spirit that would invite war;
From which lessons he would all one draw
To grace this world with calm known at night
When the world does in deep sleep alight.
From a distant land I grieve and stroke
Daddy's obelisk and would he woke
Up to have these words his eyes caress
Before he takes this prolong recess…!

Farewell IV

17-20/10/10

I'd have liked to think 'twas just a bad dream
Made me plunge in love like kids in a stream
Just to find it was nothing but lava
Destined to burn up any who lover
Professes they were just to wake up in
This river with venom full to the bream!
Is Love worth dying for, thus worth living
For in spite of the mask worn by lying
Hussies who keep off dents and dints from brave
And honest hearts they would make of their slave?
True! Life reserves surprises that abound
But not the odium that would love drag aground
Bound to that bad dream of my thoughts I hate
Here present that others muse on as fate.

Farewell V

My eyes dropped in a pit six feet deep
Dad's remains welcomed them not a death sheep
Yet, my life source does prick the eyes so hard
Me in want with my mouth drooped wide a yard!
Rocked by this pit's content, thrown in a feat,
I here on these grounds miss the grain of wheat
And hope for rebirth and bloom far afield
By a grave in which none ever needs a shield
Long after these eyes on the man did feast
With no thoughts of the fate of man nor beast
Where one drives home tears, the other relish
Not tear that's brought by famine but anguish
As fallen eyes in the pit remedy
Not needles grown at heart by tragedy.

Farewell VI

Dad would not speak nor sing; he only mused
As he shipped himself out with none amused.
I turn my ears to his musings to hear
Them project in this ride one needs no fear
Just as he'd done to teach to write on slates
That our ends should shake no tectonic plates
But take heed this were a gentle motion
To a land so still with no commotion,
Remote from this, where our hairs stand on strands
Safe when we take a goner down with bands
Drumming him goodbye while he lies down mute
After he's quit this world of disrepute
A shroud covers the little ones he'd taught
To drop their hats and face the draught he'd brought.

Farewell VII

I thought I'd rather not think dad this year.
Twenty one years gone! His voice? I still hear
Shining the light on my way to wisdom
By which dad swore would serve my kind freedom;
The one I await to bloom and blossom
In their jail house while they squeeze out ransom.
Just before daddy jumped out of his bag
To me, he brandished their sleazy filthy rag
And ignited this quest for refinement
That has turned me away from deployment
And have my eyes open to tranquility
To front their rage with equanimity
For my calm never to know privation
But, how to inhale breath of liberation.

Farewell VIII

Can I bury this image on my mind?
How come? Not even when to truth blind?
He'd strained his waist to lay my foundation
Erect and tall with pride to see me born
With spring sprout brought by me, winged cherub
To his heart whose beats resound with a throb.
As he would he went, my own starts to beat
Fast with rage for a parting dad so sweet.
Yes, he's been the nectar with me the bee
Who tapped joy from his buds and drank sweet tea!
Now, he's gone with the source of my tears left
To flood my cheeks as my cry tells of theft
That broke this dam forcing questions to stream
Out. Yet, my heart knows it should with joy scream!

Marshals in the Marshes

13-14/09/10

So, in the rain forest and rice field
Our past, present and future are stuck
And our wages in a handful of grains
Trickle down to us flooding them with gains
As they smile away having their deal struck
With growers grown scarecrow behind shield?

Now? In the quagmire of this rice field
Our losses in time and strength we count not
Just as their gains do the banks overflow
To skim thin to naught and let the storm blow
Away the change a wind to us once brought
We'll reap fruits of labour with no shield.

Soon, what awaits us in the rice field
Where circles of viciousness looms over
The air in their bid to asphyxiate us
And warrant they will always fill their purse
Were we to give them our backs forever?
Are they Marshals? No! We are in this field!

May Tree

04/10/10

A bright sunny day does unwrap itself!
Child of mysterious clouds that loomed above;
A May tree book of love doth dress the shelf!
Day and Book in them cage mysteries of Jove
Wrought by the hands of the great alchemist
In his infinite knowledge and knowing
Both mysteries and realities born of mist
On the path of warriors with no ringing
Bells to sound or mark the dangers along
These marshes on which peace of mind is farmed
To reap true love that will never be wrung
Nor broken by such forces that are armed
With bright teeth ready to laugh at heroes
Who in the dark depths of loving venture
With hopes and aspirations love echoes
And fills vales full with no place for vultures
With racing hearts by some fruits accidents
Pluck off the trajectory way before time
For May tree fruit on time would not depend
As such by vultures taken for a crime.

Class of 84

First day of school
We sat on stools
We came there to learn
This highway to earn
This bright bread ticket
Hailed certificate
We take home in numbers
But no one remembers
We are here to sow seeds
And cater for hearts' needs
With a wink to calm heat
As we'd warm our seat
With these seeds unsown
The fruit's never grown
In the heart of a desert
Are we left without dessert
Nor a rain drop of life
To keep heart beats alive
But my heart still rages
In my final stages
I'd lay my lips to steal
Kisses that my heart still
And for sure make sunrise
On this face the lone prize
We would go down the throat
Tailored to measure coat
Sweet tasting fig fruit
With me as recruit
You would twirl from tickle
As the sweet drops trickle.

A Hopeful's Day

A dark night drags home this gruesome nightmare
With the head all empty and left threadbare
The sunlight unchanged follows his aged old tradition
As hopes do sprout to brace dictates from tyrants' mansions

Sitting by such a stunted tree
Like a child with dreams to be free
With the fall of a fruit to send him wild
After he's stood the mess tyrants have piled

Year in year out drifting away
All hopes as well being swept away
Under this tree crushed stunted
By tyrants' weight subjected

The oceans in them with dryness bloom
The streams run to their core and leave gloom
To light up the hopeful's day
A drudge without any pay

And tyrants smile their hearts beat
To set graveyards free to bleed
When gangsters strive in our mansions
Just as outside springs starvation

Sun dried on sand, this people lament;
Tyrants' gift to them for enjoyment
And one day lament will make way
Give it to their breezeless bunker stay

What thinking drives the hopeful to this?
None would ever out of thirst drink piss!
But all at some point dreamt of bliss
On which day they'll steal a fun kiss!

Hope hopeful hope
See cupful scope
With the night in arrogance striding
To brighten thought of nightmare looming

Above tomorrow's sky burning and scalding
To fade along the way when falls the evening
From whose bosom rises a smile of constellation
Hopefuls copy in innocence for consolation.

Spare Me

I have fallen in love a zillion times!
Each zillion time I have heard these bells' chimes.
They chime as would creepy-crawly rattle
Whence I would I'd fallen for the prattle;
Not at sea where serpents stream in and out
And inject venom in men in a bout
Of madness buckled up where rages storm
Behind their split tongues to strike so would bombs
And tint spotlessness born each day of Rose
Beautiful, beautiful Rose, spare me Rose!

Portuguese Lobster

Lobsters? These we are?
With us cast in these nets?
Their whips we must take
With sealed mouths as we're laid
In ambush to untrap
The like of Von Trappe
Who for sunrise runs
Over the ranges
To avoid the icy cold hands of death
Yet, drags none down while he waits his last breath.
They've made us lobsters, we must say!
We've made ourselves crabs, we must say!
This curtain must be on blame game drawn
Then joy shall we hug, take and wear her crown!

Won't Sink in Sync

Mum bent over with me on her back!
In the fields she shovels with a hoe!
And as I ride high on this horseback
I know not I add to the stones
These stones she shovels with same hands
Firm to grip and hold me not to sink
Where life she shine not a piece of cake
And gives the relay baton I take
Ne'er to savour cake on armchair
But for young me to get off the chair
And should with her in her aches slip in sync
On this road of life I plod and won't sink.

With the Sails Set

My breath joins the wind
My bone goes to fiends
As my breath does sail
So does a fiend fail
In his dream I'd moan
My bones one with stone.

In the wind, my breath
Sojourns without bread
And laughs at my foes
Who'd slaved for my woes;
My breath move flowers
And gives them showers.

With my bones at rest
Their dream of arrest's
Shattered and buried
They had not harried
Their acrid lesson
Down my throat this soon!

Where the Ravens Gloat

To think what one shall think
Down in the grave would make shrink?
Not where the tentacles of my angst
Shall by peace lie with friends left in trance!

To let thoughts of where I'd go
Stand on my way like a foe?
That's the titan I'd defy without fear;
His fall to my eyes shall not bring a tear.

To lose sight of these hideous band
Stars would leave their footprints on sand?
My take? A crime against humanity
That scars the face of my humility!

To dread a soaring vulture
And hide home hopes and future?
I would have self destruct with a noose
Or flung away some broken hearts in booze!

To think a heart in the grave
Rots and with such excuse slave?
I'd rather mine rot in the battle field
Wherein my hardihood will make my shield.

To kiss and hug innocence
With the back against nonsense?
Would be to sell a conscience clean and pure
With this plague of tyrants without a cure.

To hail blood mongers for gold
Just to leave us in the cold?
Is a mission only ravens endorse
For their Viking ancestors spoke Old Norse.

To counter gangsters with bold
Moves would expurgate the mold?
Would open goons' new roads to show their might
And nab what they will and uphold our plight.

To take the hatchet and spears
And lay to rest without fears?
Goons won't let happen! We must beg for alms!
And if we want not, they would deal us arms!

Till Apocalypse would might
Ever stand in lieu of right?
That's a thing I'd never be forgiven
For kicking with life and sparing ravens!

Brides of Gold

Those fair ladies are gold rings on pigs' snouts!
Have they hearts? Yes! One you'd not plug with words!
Shackles of sort? The Lord's altars unchain
And set the just free from their thorny lane;
Thorny lane on which they'd see barefooted
Me or you with their deep rooted hatred
And flaming desires blown up in bomb blasts
Just to spin us around and stop our last
Word which must not swim out of our big mouths.
They have bright light? Must we follow like moths?
Their light of darkness we'd stay away from
And rather they beat us their drummers' drum
Trashed in anger in their show of displaced
Mine digging; yet, would not our joy replace!

This Dark World…!

To be a mother
You'd need a backbone
An iron strong backbone
To carry children
Who'd pride in their ride,
A cozy ride on
The love and support
A loving mother
Rushes to give them;
Sweet honey tasting
Love they can't deny;
This from my mother
I took and revel
In with a broad smile!
In a world so dark
Everyman craves might
To crush us native
Sons whose parents' mite
And love do bring mirth,
Not mighty misery
At the heart planted
By sick might cravers.

P5 and 8

We see men wash hands in blood
And on their knees rest
The rest of their life
To still their sour conscience
And blur their picture of saintlessness

We take a stab from the side
From the sight of such trees whose leaves
Would mask their shame,
They've made their fame,
And leave trees to kiss the ground
And sing as they're pushed around
With their songs' talks of worthless fight
To birth pricks in which they believe

With such trinkets stained with blood
That's all they've known best
And have made their drive
Whose crises of conscience
Jump into our world with meek boldness.